KT-557-114

THE VIKINGS

Jackie Gaff

CONTENTS

This is a Parragon Book
First published in 2002

Parragon
Queen Street House
4 Queen Street
Bath BA1 1HE, UK

Copyright © Parragon 2002

Produced by

David West  Children's Books
7 Princeton Court
55 Felsham Road
Putney
London SW15 1AZ

All rights reserved. No part of this publication may
be reproduced, stored in a retrieval system, or
transmitted by any means, electronic, mechanical,
photocopying, recording or otherwise, without the
prior permission of the copyright holder.

British Library Cataloguing-in-Publication Data

A catalogue record for this book is available from
the British Library.

ISBN 0-75257-824-3

Printed in Dubai

Designers
Julie Joubinaux, Rob Shone

Illustrators
James Field, Mike Lacey (SGA)

Cartoonist
Peter Wilks (SGA)

Editor
James Pickering

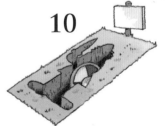

VIKING RAIDERS

ᚱᚢᛁᚾᛏᛖᚠᛖᛗᛁᛒᚱᛁᛦᛁᛏᚠᛁᛦᚾᛁᛗᛦᛏᚾᛁᚠᛁᛦᚾᛁᛗᛦᛈᚲᚱᚢᛁᚾᛏᛖᚠᛖᛗᛁ

ON 8 JUNE 793, a band of Viking warriors landed their warships on the small island of Lindisfarne, off England's northeastern coast. They were about to carry out the first Viking raid we know of – attacking the island's monastery, killing many of the monks, and stealing their treasure. For the next 300 years of the Viking age, Viking warriors were to terrorise countries throughout Europe.

YOU MUST BE JOKING!
Viking raids on England began to tail off after 1066, when the Norman-French ruler William the Conqueror invaded England and took power. William was descended from the Viking chieftain Rollo, who settled in France in the 10th century.

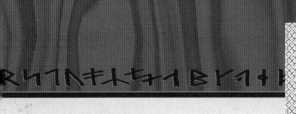

Death and destruction
The Viking raiders killed some monks at Lindisfarne by drowning or the sword. Many of the survivors were kidnapped, to be taken back to the Viking homelands and sold as slaves.

THE VIKING WORLD
The Viking homelands were in Scandinavia, in the countries we now call Denmark, Norway and Sweden. The Vikings were tremendous travellers – raiding, conquering or settling in many European lands, as well as trading goods far and wide.

CAN YOU BELIEVE IT?
Viking raiders looted the French city of Paris.

YES. In 845, the French tried to stop the raids by paying the Viking chieftain Ragnar 3,000 kilograms of silver.

THE SIGHT OF A FULLY ARMED **VIKING WARRIOR** in a battle charge was enough to strike fear into the heart of all but the bravest of opponents. The Vikings fought with everything from bows and arrows to battle axes and spears. But a warrior's favourite weapon was the double-edged sword he used to hack at his enemy's arms or legs.

CAN YOU BELIEVE IT?
Viking warriors wore horned helmets.

NO. Their helmets often had eye- and nose-guards, but no horns. They were made of metal or leather.

Protective clothing
Most Vikings carried a wooden shield and wore armour to protect themselves from their opponents' weapons. Wealthy men could afford a chainmail shirt, while others wore a padded leather jacket.

YOU MUST BE JOKING!

The scariest Viking warriors fought like mad men and were called berserkers. A really wild berserker would charge into battle without armour, howling like a wolf, and even biting his shield in his fury.

SWORD OF HONOUR

Each Viking warrior had to dress and arm himself, so the richer he was, the better quality his armour and weapons. The richest warriors had beautifully decorated swords forged by skilled weapon-smiths.

THE CHIEF REASON the Vikings were able to travel far and wide was because they were superb sailors and shipbuilders. They built many kinds, from small boats for rowing or fishing on rivers and lakes, to sea-going ships. But the Vikings' most famous vessels are the speedy longships they used on raiding voyages.

Long and lovely
At about 28 metres long, a large longship wasn't much bigger than a modernday schooner. It could carry 50 warriors. Longships could be rowed or sailed, and they were steered with a large oar at the stern (back).

CAN YOU BELIEVE IT?
Viking sailors used a compass to find their way.

NO. They navigated by watching the position of the Sun and stars in the sky.

BUILDING A LONGSHIP

Longships were usually made of oak, with the keel and mast each carved from a single tree trunk.

The sides were built from overlapping planks. The flattish base allowed the ship to sail in shallow coastal waters or up rivers.

YOU MUST BE JOKING!

The prow at the front of a longship was often carved to look like the head of a fierce dragon. The ship's sail was the dragon's wings, and the oars, its legs.

ᚱᚢᛁᚾᛖᛏᛖᚨᛁ ᛒᚱᛁᛏ ᛖᛏᚨᛁ ᛏᛏᚨᛁᛏᛏᚨᛁᛏ ᛖᛁᚾᚱᚢᚱᚢᛁᚾᛖᛏᛖᚨᛁ

DESPITE THEIR FEARSOME reputation, most Viking travellers were explorers searching for new lands to settle and farm, or traders hunting foreign markets for their goods. Viking explorers were the first Europeans to reach Iceland and Greenland. And in about the year 1000, a Viking called Leif Ericsson became the first foreigner to set foot in North America.

American dream Viking settlers from Greenland followed Leif Ericsson's route to America and tried to set up home there. They didn't stay long, though – they were driven away by the Native Americans.

ᛁᛒᚱᛁᛖ ᛏᛏᚨᛁᛏᚱᚾᛖᚨᚱᚢᚱᚢᛁᚾᛖᛏᛖᚨᛁ

YOU MUST BE JOKING!
No one is certain when or where Leif Ericsson landed in America. However, the remains of a Viking settlement have been found on the Canadian coast, at a place called L'Anse aux Meadows.

ᛁᛒᚱᛁᛖ ᛏᛏᚨᛁᛏᚱᚾᛖᚨᚱᚢᚱᚢᛁᚾᛖᛏᛖᚨᛁ

ᛁᛖᛒᚱᛖᛏᚨᛁᛏᚱᚾᛖᚨᚱᚢᚱᚢᛁᚾᛖᛏᛖᚨᛁ   ᛏᚱᚾᛖᚨᚱᚢᚱᛁ

LIFE ON THE OCEAN WAVE

The kind of ship used by Viking settlers and traders was wider and slower than a longship. Food and possessions were packed in wooden chests, while animals and cargo were stored in the centre of the boat. Come rain or sun, sea travellers spent their days and nights on deck.

CAN YOU BELIEVE IT?
Leif's name for America was Vinland, meaning 'wine land'.

YES. But his wine was probably made from huckleberries, not grapes.

THE VIKINGS WEREN'T ONE NATION ruled over by a single king or queen. For most of the Viking age, there were lots of small communities, each headed by its own king or chieftain. From time to time, each community held its own open-air meeting called a *Thing*, to discuss important issues, settle any arguments and punish crimes. It was rather like a modernday parliament.

YOU MUST BE JOKING!
There were three main groups in Viking society – *jarls* (chieftains and nobles), *karls* (free men and women), and *thralls* (slaves). Only *jarls* and *karls* could have their say at a *Thing*.

Greatest Thing on Earth
The largest Thing was held by the Vikings who settled in Iceland. It was called the Althing, and it took place every year at a huge plain called Thingvellir.

WOMEN'S RIGHTS

Unlike most other women of the time, Viking women were allowed to own their own land and property, and to keep control of it if they married. When their menfolk set off raiding, trading or exploring, the women would take over the running of the family farm or business.

CAN YOU BELIEVE IT?
Murderers had to pay a fine to their victim's family.

Yes. It was a sum of money called a *wergeld*.

THE VIKINGS BELIEVED their gods and goddesses lived in a community, too. The king of the Viking gods was Odin, and he was also the god of war, wisdom and poetry. His wife, Frigg, was the goddess of the home, and his son, Thor, was the god of thunder. The god of farming was Frey, while his sister, Freyja, was the goddess of love, battle and death.

Frey

Frigg

Odin

Sleipnir

CAN YOU BELIEVE IT?
Thor was the Vikings' favourite god.

YES. His symbol was a hammer, and people often wore a hammer pendant as a lucky charm.

Riders in the sky

The Vikings believed that many of their gods and goddesses rode across the sky, on horseback or in chariots. Odin's horse, Sleipnir, had eight legs!

Freyja

Thor

WORSHIPPING ONE GOD

By the end of the Viking age, most Vikings had converted to Christianity – giving up the old gods and goddesses for the one God of the Christian church. Beautiful wooden churches were built throughout Scandinavia.

YOU MUST BE JOKING!

The Vikings also believed in magical giants and dwarves. The dwarves were famous for their skill in working with gold, silver and jewels – and for their greed for power and beautiful women!

15

DAILY DRESS

STYLES CHANGED VERY LITTLE during the Viking age, and everyone wore the same basic outfits – although richer people could afford better quality cloth and jewellery. Viking women wore a long shift-dress under a pinafore-like tunic, with a shawl over the top when they went outdoors. Men wore a belted tunic over an undershirt and trousers. Cloaks kept people warm in winter.

YOU MUST BE JOKING!

Viking women spun and wove all the cloth, and sewed all the clothes for their families. Cloth was woven on a tall loom which stood against one of the walls inside the longhouse.

Trusty treasures

Jewellery was used to fasten clothes as well as for decoration. Women used a pair of oval brooches in front of their pinafore to attach the shoulder straps. A string of beads often hung between the brooches.

HAIRY HEADLINES

The Vikings loved long hair. Men often grew theirs shoulder-length, while women's was even longer. Men also let their beards grow, and sometimes even plaited the hair. Women's hair was usually plaited or tied up in a knot, while married women wore a headdress or a scarf.

CAN YOU BELIEVE IT?
The Vikings had ironing boards.

YES. Cloth was stretched over a smooth board and rubbed with a glass ball.

WHETHER THEY SETTLED ABROAD or stayed in their homelands, most Vikings lived by farming. Farmers grew barley, oats, rye and wheat, as well as some vegetables and fruit. They kept all sorts of animals, too – chickens, geese, cows, goats, pigs, sheep and horses. Ordinary families would all work together to run the farm, while slaves did the hard work for wealthier farmers.

YOU MUST BE JOKING!
Some Viking buildings had roofs made of turf, while others were thatched, or shingled with wooden tiles. Walls might be made of stone or wood. The Vikings built with whatever materials were handy.

Home sweet home
Farming families lived in a big building called a longhouse. Larger farms had outbuildings for animals and to store food. There was also a smithy for making and mending tools and weapons.

FISHY BUSINESS
There was little good land for farming in the far north of Scandinavia, so the Vikings who lived there hunted whales, seals and walruses for their meat. Whale bones were carved into tools, and whale oil was used to fuel lanterns.

CAN YOU BELIEVE IT?
Some Vikings hunted reindeer.

YES. Huge reindeer called caribou were the main source of meat for Viking settlers in west Greenland.

LONGHOUSES WERE OFTEN smoky and smelly inside, because there was no chimney – just a hole in the roof over a large firepit. They were also fairly dark, since few homes had windows, and the only sources of light were the fire, and candles or oil lamps. The fire was mainly for cooking and heating. In winter, it was the only cosy place to sit.

Close quarters
Ordinary Vikings lived, ate and slept in the same big room. Wooden platforms along the walls were seats during the day, and beds at night.

Wooden frame

Main entrance

YOU MUST BE JOKING!
As well as meat and fish, the Vikings ate porridge, bread, eggs, cheese and vegetables – mainly cabbage, peas and onions. They were great beer drinkers, although wealthy people also drank wine imported from France and Italy.

COOKING THE DINNER

A metal pot called a cauldron hung down over the firepit and was used for cooking stews. Meat and fish might also be roasted or grilled on skewers over the fire. Bread was often baked over the fire, too, on a flat iron griddle.

Thatched or turf roof

Firepit

'Chimney' hole

Stable

Pig pen

CAN YOU BELIEVE IT?
Ordinary Vikings had wooden bowls and plates.

YES. And hollow cattle horns were used for drinking beer.

A TRADING TOWN

TOWNS WERE FEW AND FAR BETWEEN in the Viking lands, but large trading centres included Birka in Sweden and Hedeby in Denmark, as well as Dublin in Ireland and York in England. Foreign merchants came to these towns to buy Viking goods such as amber beads, animal furs and walrus-tusk ivory. In exchange, Viking traders were keen to buy silks, spices, silver and other foreign luxuries.

CAN YOU BELIEVE IT?
The Vikings paid for goods with money.

YES. Coins were being used by the 10th century. Before that goods were exchanged, or paid for with pieces of silver.

TOWN DEFENCES

The largest Viking town was the Danish port of Hedeby. Tall earth-and-timber walls surrounded the town and harbour to protect them from enemy attack. Trading towns like Hedeby were also centres for craftsmen.

YOU MUST BE JOKING!

The wealthiest Viking merchants were the slave traders. Some slaves were prisoners captured in raids, but most were peasants kidnapped in eastern Europe. All were sold to the highest bidder.

Viking traders
The Swedish Vikings travelled great distances in search of goods to trade. They navigated the great rivers of Russia, eventually reaching Constantinople in today's Turkey.

MUCH OF THE VIKING HOMELANDS in Scandinavia was the kind of steep mountain country that's very difficult to travel through. Most people lived on low ground where there was good rich soil for farming – by lakes, along the coast, or around sea inlets called fjords. In the summer, getting around was easiest by boat or ship. Things were very different, though, when the long cold winter covered the land in snow and ice.

Snow mobility
Many lakes and rivers froze over during winter, so people switched to skis or skates, or rode in a wooden sledge pulled by horses or oxen.

YOU MUST BE JOKING!
Skis were invented in Scandinavia. A picture scratched into a rock in Norway more than 10,000 years ago shows a man on two long skis with high pointed tips.

HORSING ABOUT

The Vikings loved horses and used them for riding and as pack animals for carrying possessions. When the weather was good enough, wagons were pulled by horses or by oxen. Viking wagons had round bottoms, and looked rather like a huge half-barrel.

CAN YOU BELIEVE IT?

Viking skates were made from metal.

NO. Skates were made from animal bones tied under the wearer's boots.

WINTER WAS A GOOD TIME to snuggle up around the fire and listen to poems and stories. The Vikings loved tales about the lives and battles of great rulers and warriors. These tales were called sagas, and they were told from memory. They weren't written down until the early 13th century, after the Viking age ended.

Professional poets
Kings and chieftains often had their own professional poet and storyteller, called a skald. The skald composed poems and sagas to entertain the ruler and his court.

YOU MUST BE JOKING!
Viking sagas were true stories, about the lives of real people. The Saga of Eric the Red, for example, told how Leif Ericsson's brother Thorvald led an expedition to Vinland, where he was killed by Native Americans.

CAN YOU BELIEVE IT?
Viking children learned runes at school.

NO. The Vikings didn't have schools. Children stayed at home, and worked with their mother and father.

WRITING IN RUNES

One reason that sagas were told from memory was that few Vikings could read or write. The Viking alphabet was made up of letters called runes – it was called the *futhark*, after the first six runes. Messages were carved in wood, bone or stone.

ᚨ ᛒ ᚲ ᛝ ᛖ ᚠ ᚷ ᚼ ᛁ ᛚ ᛗ
a b c d e f g h i k l m

ᚾ ᛟ ᛈ ᚲ ᚱ ᛊ ᛏ ᚦ ᛉ ᛣ
n o p q r s tuvw x y z

THE VIKINGS DIDN'T SPEND all their free time quietly sitting around listening to sagas, of course. Viking men loved proving how rough and tough they were by taking part in wrestling matches and swimming and rowing races. Another popular activity was watching a horse-fight. The stallions were specially bred and people laid bets on the winner.

Keep fit class
Sports such as wrestling weren't simply an occasion for showing off how strong you were. They were also a way for Viking men to keep themselves fit and ready for the next raid or battle.

CAN YOU BELIEVE IT?
Viking board games were a peaceful way of passing time.

NO. People got very worked up over them, and games often ended in a fight.

WAR GAME

One of the Vikings' favourite board games was called *hnefatafl*. There were two players, each with an army of warriors. The red army had 12 warriors and a king, while the white army had 24 warriors, but no king. The white player's aim was to capture the red king.

YOU MUST BE JOKING!

Even boys practised fighting in their free time, using wooden swords so they didn't hurt each other too badly. Children also had dolls, and played a bat-and-ball game called *kingy bats*.

VIKINGS WERE BURIED in their best clothes, along with food and their most precious possessions, because people believed that the dead needed these things in the next world, the Afterlife. A farmer's wife might be buried with her spinning tools and a barrel of milk. A merchant would have his weighing scales, and a warrior, his sword.

Buried treasure
In 1903, people found a large Viking grave at Oseberg, Norway. Inside was a beautifully carved ship, with the bodies of a queen and her maid inside, along with a fine wagon, sledges and furniture, as well as tapestries and cooking pots.

ᛁᛒᛁᛏᛁᚠᛈᛋᛁᛏᚠᛁᛘᚴᚱᛋᛁᚾᛏ

CAN YOU BELIEVE IT?
Animals were sometimes killed and buried with their owner.

YES. One Viking king was buried with six dogs, twelve horses and even a peacock.

ᛁᛒᛁᛏᛁᚠᛈᛋᛁᛏᚠᛁᛘᚴᚱᛋᛁᚾᛏ

YOU MUST BE JOKING!

For a warrior, the greatest honour was to die bravely in battle. The Vikings believed that warriors joined Odin in his heavenly home Valhalla, where they spent their days fighting and nights feasting.

ROYAL SEND OFF

The most splendid burials were given to dead kings, queens and chieftains. Some were buried in a longship, to carry them to the Afterlife. To speed the journey, the ship was sometimes set on fire.

INDEX